STORIES FROM HOME

The Monologue Collection

Yvonne Marie Montoya

Montoya Publishing

Copyright © 2025 Yvonne Marie Montoya

All rights reserved

No part of this book may be reproduced, or stored in a retrieval system, or transmitted in any form or by any means, electronic, mechanical, photocopying, recording, or otherwise, without express written permission of the publisher.

ISBN: 979-8-9987629-1-8

Cover design and illustrations by: Wesley Fawcett Creigh
Author Photo by: Baylie MacRae
Library of Congress Control Number: 2025913478
Printed in the United States of America

For Buddy el hijo de mi alma

In loving memory of Dad Juan "Johnny" Sebastian Montoya Sena and Granmita María Aurelia Luján

Nuevo México querido, no haga caso al mitote, entre Indios y Americanos, toditos semos coytotes.

TRADITIONAL NUEVOMEXICANO VERSE

CONTENTS

Title Page
Copyright
Dedication
Epigraph
Preface
Stories from Home
Tecolote	1
Mestiza Mulata de Analco	3
Siglos. Sueños. Sefarad.	18
Deslenguadas	27
Braceros	35
Pajarito	40
Unspoken	50
Cómo eres	53
Querencia	57
Acknowledgement	63
About The Author	75

| Books By This Author | 77 |
| Stories from Home | 79 |

PREFACE

"My dad was a storyteller."

Those are the first five words that open the two hour evening length live contemporary dance performance *Stories from Home*. *Stories from Home* is a series of dances that are the physical embodiments of the oral traditions of Northern New Mexico. This collection of dances represents stories inspired by my father and were created for my son in honor of our ancestors, our querencia, and our deep, deep Nuevomexicano roots. This is an artistic interpretation of my family's histories and stories inspired by and based on, but not beholden to, historical accuracies as time is not linear in this storytelling experience. I am delighted to share my family's stories and cultural traditions with you.

I began creating *Stories from Home* after my father passed away in 2015; compelled to continue his storytelling tradition for my son. The work is inspired by oral histories I did with my great-grandmother, grandmother, maternal great-aunts, and father and explores themes of love, family, and home. *Stories From Home* is a vessel for personal and specific tales, while also offering a broader look at various cultural traditions throughout the Southwest.

There are a total of twelve dances in *Stories from Home*. Of those twelve dances, eight contain accompanying written narratives, stories in the form of monologues, based on and inspired by the theme of the dances. This book is the collection of the eight written stories that accompany the dances. These writings are the heart and soul of *Stories from Home*.

Why Share The Stories In A Book?

Very few of the written stories or monologues from *Stories from Home* are shared in their entirety during the dance performance. In fact, of the eight written stories, only two, *Tecolote*, the opening monologue, and *Pajarito*, are shared in their entirety. In

Querencia, the closing monologue, all but one paragraph is performed on stage. Artistic readings of *Mestiza Mulata de Analco* and *Deslenguadas* are also performed on stage, but the written stories are not shared in their entirety. Rather, shorter versions are shared. And with *Unspoken*, excerpts of the written story appear in the animation that precedes the dance. Regarding the remaining four dances, none of the written stories are shared on stage.

During *Stories from Home* storytelling workshops, the opening monologue *Tecolote* and the writing for *Como Eres* are usually performed in their entirety. In the case of a special mini performance of *Siglos. Sueños. Sefarad.*, that monologue is performed in its entirety before the dance.

What Came First, The Writing Or The Dance?

In most cases, I wrote the accompanying stories (monologues) prior to or in the initial phase of the choreographic process. I wrote these stories to help gather my thoughts and narrow down which aspects of the story I thought were the most important to embody and share.

Siglos. Sueños. Sefarad., *Pajarito*, *Unspoke*n, *Mestiza Mulata de Analco,* and *Querencia* were all written before beginning the choreographic process.

In fact, the monologue of *Pajarito* was not initially intended to be performed on stage. With *Pajarito*, I created the movement prior to the composer Samuel Peña writing the score for the dance. During an end-of-rehearsal work-in-progress showing, without music, I read the monologue while the dancers moved. The feedback from the group gathered for the work-in-progress showing in early 2021, including that of composer Peña, strongly supported including the monologue in the performance.

For *Mestiza Mulata de Analco*, multiple writings informed the initial artistic process, including some handwritten lines of poetry and prose that are now lost to time and other writings that are not ready for publication. Elements of the initial writings that informed the choreography created by Ruby Morales during the Makers Space Experience (MSE)

Residency at Keshet Dance & Center for the Arts in Albuquerque, NM in 2019 are included in the monologue performed on stage. Although the monologue was edited into its final form after the dance was complete.

The writing for *Braceros*, *Deslenguadas*, and *Tecolote* occurred after the dances were choreographed. In this case, the writings serve as a reflection of the dances.

In choreographing these stories, I did my best to only share in words that which could not be said through movement.

Stories From Home

Stories from Home was years in the making. I began the initial choreographic process in July 2017 during a Parent Artist residency at SPACE on Ryder Farm in Brewster, NY where I incubated Braceros and the re-work of *Deslenguadas*. *Stories from Home* was originally set to soft premiere September 2020 on Kennedy Center's MStage, a performance canceled due to the pandemic.

After some pandemic setbacks and detours, and an expansion of the work to include *Pajarito*, *Stories from Home* premiered October 27-28, 2023 at GALA Hispanic Theatre in Washington, D.C. At the time of this writing, the show is currently touring throughout the Southwest and beyond.

This book contains the writings of *Stories from Home*, the writings that are the inspiration behind the dances. The writings appear in the order that dances are performed during the evening length show. The book features two versions of *Mestiza Mulata de Analco* and *Deslenguadas*. One is the shorter artistic version performed on stage and the others are the longer versions, the full stories behind the dances. *Querencia* includes an additional paragraph not performed on stage. But as the additional writing is only a paragraph, I did not include two versions of this writing.

The book concludes with acknowledgements including my deep thank yous and gratitudes followed by the program notes from *Stories from Home*, including artistic credits and funders credits.

STORIES FROM HOME

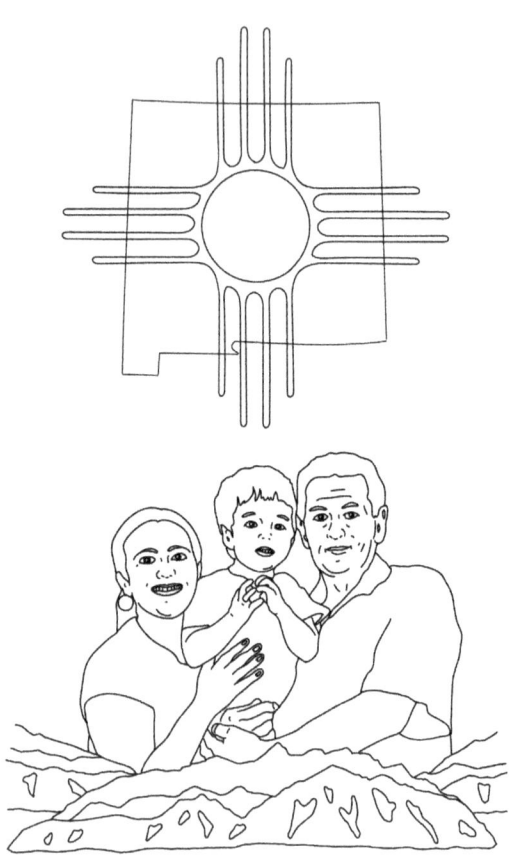

TECOLOTE

My dad was a storyteller. He loved to talk and tell jokes and could always come up with a story about my childhood or great uncles who I never had the chance to meet. My father was so skilled in the Nuevomexicano or northern New Mexican art of storytelling and oral tradition that my brothers and sister and I never knew which stories were true and which were highly embellished. When he passed away in 2015, it was a tremendous loss. All the stories and the memories of generations past went with him. I felt incredibly sad for my son Buddy, who was seven at the time of my father's passing. He is growing up away from New Mexico and its all encompassing cultures and traditions that wrap around you and seep into your soul. When my dad died, the connections to the stories were gone as well. I realized that it was my turn to pick up the tradition of gathering and sharing family stories as my father once did. I needed to share these stories with my son. I decided to continue my father's tradition of storytelling in a language I love most, the language of dance. This is the inspiration behind *Stories from Home*.

I am Yvonne Montoya. The daughter of Juan Sebastian Montoya Sena and Darlene Roybal. The granddaughter of Adolfo Montoya, María Rosina Sena, Eduardo Horacio Roybal and María Graciola Roybal. And the great-grand daughter of Ricarte Bernardo Montoya, Margarita Montoya, Mariano Victoriano Sena, Jesusita Padilla, Antonio María Roybal, María Saloma Gómez, José Cesario Roybal and María Aurelia Luján. And this is my story.

MESTIZA MULATA DE ANALCO

This dance is dedicated to the empty branches on my family tree, especially my many grandmothers, whose *casta** classifications were listed in official Spanish colonial documents instead of their names. Although I will never know my grandmothers' names and stories, I know that they are me.

The Version Performed On Stage

Granmita. María Aurelia Luján. Bisabuela.

4 | STORIES FROM HOME

Tita. Virginia Quintana. Tatarabuela.

Nombre desconocido. Genízara. Trastatarabuela.

Shimásání. Manuelita Yazzie. 5th Great-Grandmother.

Miguela Quintana. India de la casa. Ancestra.

María de Hinojos. Coyota. Criada. Ancestra.

María Lugarda Hurtado de Salazar. Coyota. Criada. Ancestra.

Agustina de Arbaca. India. Ancestra.

Isabel de Pedraza. India. Ancestra.

Mestiza Mulata de Analco

Mestiza Mulata de Analco

Mestiza Mulata de Analco

Mestiza Mulata de Analco

What was your name?

Where were you from?

And what was it like living in Santa Fe, when Analco was a Tlaxcalteca village?

Mestiza Mulata de Analco

The priest didn't even bother to write down your name.

Do I look like you?

    Mija.

Do I have your eyes?

> *'Jita.*

Where are you in me?

Mestiza Mulata de Analco

I cannot find my great-grandmother's families. Will you help me?

Jesusita Padilla, Felicita Montoya, Virginia Quintana, Manuelita Yazzie, Miguela Quintana, María de Hinojos, María Lugarda Hurtado de Salazar, Agustina de Arbaca, Ysabel de Pedraza.

Words carry weight here.

Carved into the land like acequias filled with my Granmita's, my Tita's, my Grandmother's, and my tears.

Mestiza Mulata de Analco.

Were you a criada?

A genízara.

Two of my 11th great-grandmothers were criadas.

Coyotas from Zuñi Pueblo.

Taken by Apaches.

As fate would have it, the woman that owned them also happened to be my 12th great-grandmother.

One of my great-grandmothers owned two of my other great-grandmothers.

One of my great-grandmothers owned two of my other great-grandmothers.

One of my great-grandmothers owned two of my other great-grandmothers.

Mestiza Mulata de Analco.

Do you know who I am?

'Hija.

Centuries of stories gone. Erased.

Living embodiments of complexity.

Love.

Expulsion.

Conquest.

Rape.

Yo soy la 'jita de las mujeres de esta tierra.

I am the 13th great-granddaughter of the Mestiza Mulata de Alaco.

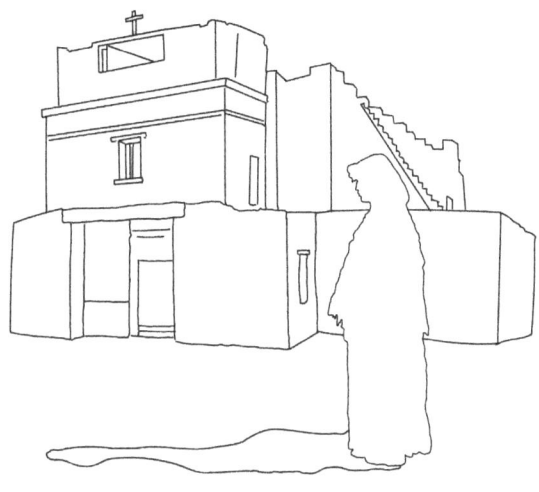

* * *

Mestiza Mulata De Analco

My dad's skin was brown. He would often put his arm next to mine and compare our skin colors. He would tell me, laughing and joking as he always did "'*Jita*, why are you so light? Look at you! Look at that skin! I am going to have to have a talk with your mom because I am not sure you are my child! You need to get some sun on those arms and legs!" Yes, it was a joke, but it broke a piece of my heart every time he did this. I loved my dad so much and I wanted to be just like him, to look just like him. As a child, I could not understand why, despite my efforts of sitting in the sun, my skin would never match the color of my dad's. According to my dad's story, he said he got his skin color from his grandmother, who was Mescalero Apache from the Vaughn or Ft. Sumner area of New Mexico. My great-grandmother's name was Jesusita Padilla. I never had the chance to meet her and I have not been able to find any records of her childhood or records of her parents. Although I want to believe my dad's story, I do not know where she is from.

My maternal grandfather tells a story about his great-grandmother whose last name was originally Yazzie. There is no record of her or her family that I can find. But Grandpo says that when the Navajo Long Walk stopped in Santa Fe, mi granma Manuelita, who was a child at the time, was sent to Santa Clara Pueblo where she lived until she married my 4th great grandfather Primitivo Gómez. My 5th great-grandmother

mi granma Manuelita

on the Navajo Long Walk

as a child.

I wonder who granma Manuelita's parents and family were and what happened to them after they arrived at Fort Sumner,

if they arrived at Fort Sumner.

I wish I knew their names.

Growing up, there was a recurring argument at my home that would happen every so often. It would go like this. My mom would insist that we were 100% Spanish, which of course is not true. Then my dad, often flummoxed, would counter by exclaiming that his grandmother was Native American. He would tell my mom that when the Spanish came that they didn't bring women. As the argument escalated, he would say to her, look at my skin, look at my face, look at my chest, using his skin color and lack of beard and chest hair as an embodied testament to make his point. His retorts fell on deaf ears and the argument would occur again months later.

Turns out, my dad was right.

> *Ysabel de Pedraza, one of my 13th maternal great grandmothers, was born 1593 . Her father Juan de Pedraza was a man from Cataluña Spain. He was also a member of the Oñate expedition to colonize present-day New Mexico. Her mother was an unmarried woman listed in church records as "India."*
>
> *My 14th maternal great grandmother. A Native woman. Nameless. Her name and place of birth were left off of the written historical record.*

Casta was a racial, social hierarchy and classification system used in colonial Spain. When I saw my great-grandmother listed as "India," I was horrified to see that the priests in charge of keeping these records didn't even bother to write down the name of my great-grandmothers.

> *Capitán Cristóbal Baca, one of my 12th maternal great grandfathers was born 1635 . His father was Alonso de Baca. His mother was a woman whose casta is listed as Mestiza Mulata de Analco. My thirteenth great-grandparents, they were not married. Of course not. I wonder what was she to him? Lover? Criada? Genízara? My 13th maternal great grandmother. Nameless. Her*

children's names were written into history. Hers was not. Mestiza Mulata de Analco. Analco - Tlaxcalteca village turned genízaro village turned tourist attraction.

In 2018, I had my genealogy done. Given that New Mexico was sparsely populated and relatively isolated for many centuries and the fact that the Spanish Catholic church took excellent records, my family genealogy was a bit easier to trace back through time.

María de Zamora, one of my 12th maternal great grandmothers, was accused of witchcraft. Born in Barrio San Sebastian Tezcoco Mexico City in 1573. Daughter of Pedro Zamora and Agustina de Abarca. Some say she was a mestiza. Others an India. All say she was an original colonizer of New Mexico. Seems things back home were always complicated.

When I opened the genealogy in my email, I was very excited and eager to see what I was going to find. What surprised and shocked me most were that many large branches of my family tree were missing. Empty. Blank. With no history or names.

Tracing the empty branches, I noticed a pattern. The vast majority led back to a grandmother, with no record of her parents or grandparents.

> *One of my 12th paternal great grandfathers is from Ohkay Owingeh (formerly known as San Juan) Pueblo and he fought against the colonizers during the Pueblo Revolt. I do not know his name.*
>
> *Juana de la Cruz Apodaca, one of my 12th paternal great grandmothers was taken during the Pueblo Revolt and lived at Ohkay Owingeh Pueblo from 1680 until 1717 when her family members returned to New Mexico with the Reconquista and recognized her at the Pueblo. At the age of 12, Juana de la Cruz gave birth at Ohkay Owingeh to my 11th great-grandmother Maria de Apodaca. I wonder how that child was conceived. And I wonder how these grandmothers felt as they were taken away from the Pueblo after 37 years.*

Then I began to notice something that brought me to tears. At the end of some of these empty branches were listed casta classifications "*india, mestiza, coyota*" instead of the names of my grandmothers.

My 12th paternal great grandmother was from Zuñi Pueblo. There is no record of her name. The story says she had three daughters with Bartolome de Salazar. Those daughters were María Lugarda Hurtado de Salazar, Isabel de Salazar Hurtado, and María Josefa de Hinojos. She also had a son with another man listed on historical records as "Indian named Venturna." The story says that my great-grandmother's three daughters were taken by Apaches and later rescued by either their father or some other man named Andres Hurtado. It is unclear who rescued them. But after their rescue, the daughters were then given to Doña Bernadina Salas y Trujillo to be raised as criadas. Called "Coyotas de Zuñi," two of the three sisters are my 11th great grandmothers. María Lugarda Hurtado de Salazar on my maternal side and María Josefa de Hinojos on my paternal side.

As fate would have it, Doña Bernadina Salas y Trujillo, the woman who owned my 11th grandmothers, also happens to be my 12th maternal great grandmother. It's all so complicated.

I cried for them. For days I cried for them. My grandmothers whose names I will never know. Indigenous women, genizaras, mestizas, women they called coyotas and mulatas.

I gathered the names that I could and held them close.

As I dug deeper into these empty branches of missing ancestors, I saw the history of New Mexico as it lives within my bones, within my veins. I saw history as it lives within me.

Colonization. The Pueblo Revolt. La Reconquista. Criadas. Genizaras. Indigenous Slavery. The Navajo Long Walk. New Mexico's past interwoven in my bones, living in my veins.

My very own complicated Nuevomexicana mestizaje.

I am at least a 23rd generation Nuevomexicana. I say at least because I know my roots run deeper, but parts of me are missing and there are grandmothers who I cannot find.

✽ ✽ ✽

*The Casta System: A porous system of racial classification in Spanish colonial society. Casta categorizations mentioned in this dance include India, Mestiza, Mulata, and Coyota/Coyotes.

Criada: From the Spanish verb criar, "to rear." Refers to Natives who were usually captured while young and raised by Spanish colonists to work in colonizers' households. A euphemism for an indentured servant.

Genízara: Detribalized Indigenous people who, through war or trade, were abducted and taken into Hispano households as laborers.

Resources

Bustamante, Adrian. "The Matter Was Never Resolved: The Casta System in Colonial New Mexico, 1693-1823." New Mexico Historical Review 66, 1991.

Gonzales, Moises, and Enrique R. Lamadrid, editors. "Nación Genízara: Ethnogenesis, Place, and Identity in New Mexico." Querencias Series, University of New Mexico Press, 2019.

Reséndez, Andrés. "The Other Slavery: The Uncovered Story of Indian Enslavement in America." Houghton Mifflin Harcourt, 2016.

Roessel, Ruth. "Navajo Stories of the Long Walk Period." 1st ed., Navajo Community College Press, 1973.

SIGLOS. SUEÑOS. SEFARAD.

How does one remember what was hidden for so long? This dance is dedicated to my Sephardic Crypto-Jewish ancestors who took refuge from the Spanish and Mexican Inquisitions in Northern New Mexico.

Sometimes the best stories are the ones kept secret.

Growing up my mom told me that Tita, my second

great grandmother, said we have relatives in Turkey. I never thought anything of it until I was at graduate school writing a thesis on New Mexico history. I mentioned it to my advising professor who immediately told me that no one from Turkey ever made their way to New Mexico. I thought it was an odd disconnect.

My great-grandmother María Aurelia Luján died 2 days before her 101st birthday. Her brother, Tío Luis, lived to be 102. A fact I randomly mentioned to my husband one Sunday afternoon. He then asked me a question that I was not anticipating. He said "Are you sure your Granmita isn't Jewish? I answered, well, you know they say that there are a bunch of Crypto-Jews in New Mexico- hahaha!, and didn't think more of it.

In 2015, the Spanish government felt bad for having expelled the Sefardic Jews from the peninsula in 1492 and passed a law offering a path to citizenship for the descendants of Sefardim. Articles referring to the law were being shared among my New Mexico friends on social media. I told my husband who, joking with me about my light skin color, asked if I was going to apply. I said no, absolutely not, why would I want to immigrate to a country who committed genocide on my indigenous ancestors and expulsion and religious persecution of my Jewish ancestors. You see, for me, it was never a question if I had Crypto-Jewish ancestors, in 2015 I was under the assumption that most Nuevomexicanos do have one or two ancestors who were Crypto-Jews. But I just thought it was one random ancestor somewhere in the distant past.

A few years passed and I saw some more social media posts about Spain and Portugal's citizenship for the descendents of Sefardim. I click on the link and immediately become overwhelmed. Even if I want to, where am I supposed to find Inquisition records of ancestors who lived over 500 years ago?? I open another link where someone compiled last names of conversos or Jews who were forcibly converted to Catholicism, and it blows my mind because it reads like a New Mexico high school yearbook. So many last names that I rarely see outside of New Mexico are on that list. Crazy coincidence, I thought.

In 2018, I met a fellow Nuevomexicana who was taking the steps to identify Sefardic ancestors and apply for Spanish citizenship. I couldn't believe that she was able to find records of ancestors who appeared on documents of the Spanish Inquisition. I asked her for the information of the person who ran her genealogy because my mom always said that we had some Jewish ancestors and maybe it would be fun to find out.

I called the Jewish Federation of New Mexico because they had a Sefardic Heritage Certificate program and I thought maybe they could help point me in the right direction. I explained to the director that I live in AZ but I am from NM and I did my genealogy recently and I am wondering if I have any Sefardic ancestors, but I can't tell from the document. She said to me "Let's see if you are related to any of the famous ones?" I thought to myself, there are famous ones???

I forwarded her my genealogy via email while we were on the phone. The first "famous" name she looked for turns up empty. Nothing. Then she says "Oh you are descended from the Carvajal family.

Yes you have Sefardic ancestors. We don't need to look any further." I hung up the phone. Who is this Carvajal family and why have I never heard of them??

> *My 10th great grandparents are Igancio Roybal y Torrado and Francisca Gómez-Robledo.*

> *My 12th great grandparents are Diego de Vera, María Ortiz de Abendaño, Jacque Santiago Goulet and Maria Elena Gallegos.*

> *My 13th great grandparents are Simón Abendaño, María de Baca Ortiz, Yvon Grolet, Marie Odoin, Juan de Greigo, María Pasquala Bernal, Bartolome Romero, Luisa López Robledo, Isabel Holguín and Juan de Vitoria Carvajal.*

> *All documented judizantes. New Mexico's Cryptojews.*

I expected to find some Sefardí ancestors. I did not expect to find so many. Nor did I expect the exquisiteness of the endogamy and arranged marriages my Crypto-Jewish family did over the centuries in a failed attempt to keep the bloodline pure. I did not expect my grandfather to tell me that they found a menorah in the house of my great-grandmother when she died. I did not expect my grandmother and mother to gift me menorahs when I found out. And I did not expect my Dad to have a handful of Sefardic ancestors either. I wished he were alive to ask him about these things.

In graduate school I read a book titled *To the Ends of the Earth: A History of the Crypto-Jews of New Mexico* by Stanley Hordes. When I read it many years ago, I did not realize that I was reading a family history. It was my Mom who noticed the connection. While visiting for a concert, she noticed the book lying on my table, picked it up, studied it for a moment and then began taking pictures of it. When I asked her what she was doing, she said that she thought the graveyard on the book cover was the El Rancho graveyard where our great-great-great-great ancestors are resting. She sent a photo to my grandmother to confirm and my mom was right. The photo on the book cover is my ancestral graveyard in El Rancho, New Mexico. Upon a second reading, I discovered that most of my Sefardic ancestors were mentioned in the book.

Little things began to make more sense. Most of my friends growing up were catholic, I was raised with no religion. I remember being told as a child if I went to church with a friend not to take the host and never to confess to a priest, but when pressed, my parents didn't explain why. And then there were those relatives in Turkey. Turkey was the Ottoman Empire when the Sefardim were expelled from the Iberian Peninsula and many Sefardim took refuge in the Ottoman Empire. Perhaps Tita was right, maybe we do have relatives in Turkey.

Even though my mother's cousins died of breast cancer because they carried the BRCA1 gene mutation, which I know is usually Askenazim but for some reason exists in New Mexico. Even though I expected to find some Sefardic great grandparents, I was blown away by the extent and depth of my Sefardim, converso, Cryptojewish ancestry. And then, my maternal grandparents shared more stories. Stories of grandmothers lighting candles around sunset on Friday nights, stories of great uncles praying at a cofradia on Fridays while the local catholic priest advised people not to go there but to come to mass instead. Death rituals of covering mirrors and wearing black for a year, menorahs in the local El Rancho catholic church. My great-grandmother's regional New Mexican Spanish vocabulary with words like "*Asina*" sounding ever so slightly like Ladino. Stories and stories and stories. I had no idea how to navigate my way through these new familial revelations. There were a few months that I wished I could return to a time where I didn't know all the details of my ancestors because it was so overwhelming.

And then I began to question where do these stories live in me? Are there ancestral memories buried somewhere deep within my bones? What connection do I have to the Sefardim? Everything seems so lost to time and forgotten.

In 2019, my son and I visited the airy and empty La Sinagoga Santa María la Blanca, in Toledo, Spain. Walking the streets of the Judería where my Sefardic ancestors might have walked, visiting a site of ancestral worship.

And I felt it. I finally felt it.

They survived.

Crossing oceans and deserts. They survived.

Despite the best efforts of Los Reyes Católicos and centuries of hiding from the Inquisitions, they survived. For me and for my son and the generations to come.

They survived yet not unchanged. For me and my son, all that remains of the religion and culture of our Sefardim ancestors are whispers from a distant past.

❋ ❋ ❋

Resource
Hordes, Stanley M. "To the End of the Earth: A History of the Crypto-Jews of New Mexico." Columbia University Press, 2005.

DESLENGUADAS

"Why don't you speak Spanish?"

The Version Performed On Stage*

My granmita, my maternal great-grandmother, María Aurelia Luján did not speak a word of English. As a child, I thought all grandparents spoke Spanish and English because mine did. I was in the 4th grade and living in West Texas when I realized that my friends' grandparents didn't speak Spanish at all.

My Granmita, my maternal Great-Grandmother, María Aurelia Luján was born in Truchas, New Mexico in 1911. One year before New Mexico became a state.

New Mexico, a state whose constitution says "All business and education should be done in both English and Spanish." My granmita, New Mexico born and raised, didn't need English in her day.

I am the first monolinugal English speaker in my family. Both of my parents' first language was Spanish.

The story goes that when my mom turned 5 years old her parents sent her to the kindergarten in Los Alamos to learn English. My mom said that after her parents sent her to the kindergarten on the hill, they never spoke to her in Spanish again.

I asked my parents why they didn't teach me Spanish.

My dad said it was because I didn't want to learn.

My mom said nothing.

My grandmother began to cry.

During World War II, the United States government began Americanization programs in non-English speaking ethnic enclaves including the French speaking populations in Louisiana, the German speaking populations in Texas, and the Spanish speaking communities throughout the Southwest including Northern New Mexico.

In elementary schools names were changed. María Graciola Clarabel became Grace, Eduardo Horaico became Eddie, Juan Sebastian became Johnny and Spanish was beaten and punished out of 5 and 6 year olds. 5 and 6 year olds whose teachers called them dirty. 5 and 6 year olds who were bullied for bringing a jar of beans and a tortilla wrapped in foil to school for lunch everyday.

My Spanish is all but gone, faded with time.

It rests with the memory of my Granmita.

* The version performed on stage also includes an excerpt from Gloria Anzaldúa's *La Nueva Mestiza's* Chapter 5 "How to Tame a Wild Tongue."

❊ ❊ ❊

Deslenguadas

My granmita, my maternal great-grandmother, María Aurelia Luján did not speak a word of English. As a child, I thought all grandparents spoke Spanish and English because mine did. I was in the 4th grade and living in West Texas when I realized that my friends' grandparents didn't speak Spanish at all.

My maternal great-grandmother, my granmita, was born in 1911 in Truchas, New Mexico. She was born one year before New Mexico became a state. New Mexico. A state whose constitution says something along the lines of "all business and education should be done in English and Spanish." My granmita, New Mexico born and raised, didn't need to speak English in her day. I am the first generation of monolingual English speakers in my family. Both of my parents' first language was Spanish. The story says that when my mom turned 5 years old, her parents sent her to the Anglo (that was the term used at the time) kindergarten in Los Alamos where she learned English. When she told me the story she said that after she went to kindergarten on the Hill, her parents never spoke to her in Spanish again.

As a teenager, I was interested in learning the history and traditions of my family. Obviously, not a lot has changed. My dad, probably tired of being questioned, told me that if I wanted to know the really old stories, I should talk to my granmita. But I didn't speak Spanish and she didn't speak English and I couldn't communicate with her beyond asking for "cakey", my family's Spanglish way of saying cake. Nonetheless, I was determined to learn Spanish, to talk to my granmita and learn her stories. I majored in Spanish literature in college with the sole goal to be able to speak with my great grandmother. I learned the language well enough to learn her recipes, her songs, and talk with her for hours and hours on end in her kitchen or garden. Sometimes, I would record our conversations so I could go back and listen to all that was missed in the moment.

I lived with my granmita one summer break while at college. She was 89 at the time and lived alone in El Rancho in her adobe house by the acequia. Her adobe house that once belonged to my 5th great-grandmother, my great-grandfather's grandmother, who gifted the couple her home. That summer, I walked with my Granmita. We picked *chimajá*. She showed me how she replastered her adobe house. I learned that the spice of New Mexico green chile for breakfast is not quenched by a hot cup of black coffee. Granmita laughed and laughed at my academic Spanish and told me I sounded like a book. And when my car broke down, she seriously advised me to get a "burro" because they were more reliable than a horse or car. She was always laughing, or singing and humming. I tried desperately to catch the nuances and regionalisms of her dialect. The last generation of monolingual Spanish speakers in my family. Was that Tewa or Ladino I heard in there? Or perhaps nothing at all.

I asked my parents why they didn't teach me Spanish. My dad said because I didn't want to learn. My mom said nothing. I asked my maternal grandmother and she began to cry.

During World War II, the United States began Americanization programs in areas of non-English speaking ethnic enclaves such as the French speaking populations in Louisiana, the German speaking populations in Texas and the Spanish speaking communities in the SW including northern NM. In elementary school, names were changed. María Graciola Clarabel became Grace, Eduardo became Eddy. Juan Sebastian became Johnny and Spanish was beaten and punished out of five and six year olds whose teacher's called them dirty. Five and six year olds who were bullied for bringing a jar of beans and a tortilla wrapped in foil to school for lunch.

Parallels and parallels to generations past. This is just the most recent version of this chapter in my story.

Having served its purpose, my Spanish is all but gone, faded with time, it rests with the memory of my Granmita.

❋ ❋ ❋

Resource

Parra, Carlos Francisco. "Lessons in Americanization: Educational Attainment and Internal Colonialism in Albuquerque Public Schools, 1879–1942." New Mexico Historical Review, 2016.

BRACEROS

In loving memory of my father Juan "Johnny" Sebastian Montoya Sena. This dance reflects the time he worked as a Bracero, a migrant farm worker, picking watermelon and cantaloupe in the fields of Southern Arizona and Southern California in the early 1960s.

Growing up, my dad would tell me stories of picking watermelon and cantaloupe with the Braceros program. He would share stories about early mornings rising before dawn, eating the hearts of watermelons, and sleeping in shacks with the roofs so poorly made that when he slept on the top bunk, he could see the stars between the wood panels that made up the roof. The youngest son in a family of seven, my dad said that when they traveled from Santa Fe to Yuma or Santa Barbara that there was no room for him to sit in the family station wagon. He had to stand up behind the driver's seat for hours on end. He told me he would peer over his dad's left shoulder and watch the road and chat with his dad. His Dad. My grandfather Adolfo Montoya. (I never met him. He died years before I was born).

My father and grandfather worked for the Bracero program. As a child, my father and his family would move between Santa Fe and a new farming town in Southern California or Southern Arizona every nine months. Between the ages of 11-14 years old my dad picked cantaloupe and watermelon in Yuma. Migrant farm worker. His experience as a migrant farmworker is a familiar story for Nuevomexicanos of generations past. The generation before my dad saw my maternal great-uncles and great-grandfather working as migrant farm workers in Colorado's beet fields, and in central Arizona. My dad and my great-uncles and great-grandfather before him would work alongside Mexican laborers, Braceros.

When shopping at the grocery store, my father would knock on every single watermelon until he found the most hollow sounding fruit. He insisted the more hollow sounding, the sweeter and juicier the watermelon would be. My mother dismissed these stories as tall tales that were untrue, but I always believed him.

When I was eighteen, I was driving my two younger brothers, ten and thirteen at the time, from Albuquerque to San Diego to visit family and, of course, go to Magic Mountain. We stopped in Tucson overnight but left for San Diego really early in the morning. On the outskirts of Yuma I saw the farm workers in rows picking in the fields. "Wake Up!" I scream to my brothers, trying my best to shake them awake with one hand on the steering wheel. "Wake up! Look! The Braceros are in the field picking and we are almost in Yuma. Look! Dad wasn't lying!"

My father was born in Mexico City in 1949. When people hear that they say, ah! Your dad is Mexican. Well, yes and no. My Dad was born and lived in Mexico City until the age of two but his parents were from Santa Fe and his grandparents were from

Santa Fe and his great-grandparents were from New Mexico, and his great-great-grandparents were from New Mexico and so on, and so on. The story says my grandfather Adolfo Montoya was in the U.S. military, I think he was a veteran. And because it was uncler to my dad, it is unclear to me, but some way or another because my grandfather was bilingual he was sent to Mexico City to help with a hoof and mouth disease outbreak in the late 1940s. That was why my paternal grandparents lived in Mexico City for a few years. So my dad was a Mexicano Nuevomexicano o Nuevomexicano Mexicano, or a New Mexican Mexican as my son sometimes self-identifes. Either way my dad's story and life taught me about the South North connection that has existed in the Southwest for centuries.

Shortly after I married my Mexican immigrant husband who I met in the borderlands of Tucson, my dad drove down to visit. We gathered at my in-laws house as my husband's maternal grandfather Miguel Angel Baldenegro-Escalante was visiting from Cananea, México. My dad began telling the stories of his time as a bracero and my grandfather in law, who had very limited mobility because of Parkinsons, proudly stood up and told my dad that he too was a bracero. The shared experience immediately connected the two men across a generation, region, across countries and across time and they began a deeper conversation about their experiences. Across the vast deserts and borders of the Southwest, we are much more connected than we think.

* * *

Resource
"1942: Bracero Program" Library of Congress.

PAJARITO

They said the mountains burned purple.

Sofía Vigil and Noberto Roybal, my 3rd maternal great grandparents, had a homestead on the Barranca Mesa on the Pajarito Plateau in Northern NM. In 1943, they were evicted from their homestead by the U.S. Government so that a top-secret facility could be built. Project Y. The Manhattan Project. The Los Alamos Scientific Laboratory on the Pajarito Plateau. The Lab that is today known as the Los Alamos National Laboratory. My maternal great-grandparents were evicted from their home so that the United States government could build the Atomic Bomb.

> *Norberto Roybal, Santa Fe Land Office Records. Date of original application January 11, 1909. Date filed July 31, 1916. Patented November 4, 1920. Patent #780148. 125 acres of land. Location: Barranca Mesa. Eastern part between Rendjia and Bayo Canyons. Isolated by a steep canyon. Access to land through that of neighbor Estanislado Gonzales, Sofia Vigil's 1st cousin.**

When looking for a site for the top-secret Manhattan Project, Robert Oppenheimer, who spent some time at the Los Alamos Boys Ranch School as a child, was looking for an isolated location that met the following criteria: one road in, one road out, a source of water, and an easily mobilized secret labor force.

> *Norberto Roybal from San Ildefonso. Age 45. Nine kids. Three room two story cabin*

> *with an iron roof near the present-day intersection of Navajo and Barranca roads in Los Alamos. Corral and two stock ponds, one made of concrete. A three wire fence. Cultivated 100 acres of corn, beans, rye, oats, peas, fodder and straw. 13 cattle, four horses, two hogs and chickens. No water supply. Dry farming. Spring for animals is 1 mile away. Permanent residence was in San Ildefonso.*

After considering a few locations, Oppenheimer chose Los Alamos, despite the lack of a water source, because of the population of potential laborers who could quietly and easily be put to work. I guess he figured that the Tewa and Spanish speaking people living in the valleys surrounding the Pajarito Plateau would be a built in labor force.

They said the mountains burned purple.

Stories. Less than 24 hours to evacuate. Stories of forced evictions by men in uniforms carrying rifles. Stories of my 3rd great uncle having to be physically removed from the Pajarito Plateau. Stories of vecinos losing everything they had, only taking with them the pots and pans that fit in their horse drawn wagons. Retreating down the hill into the valley. Leaving their homes, crops, and livestock behind. The livestock the military then used for target practice.

After my great-great-great grandparents were evicted from Barranca Mesa on the Pajarito Plateau, three generations of my family worked at the Los Alamos National Laboratory, or what the locals call "the Lab."

My maternal great-grandfather José Cesario Roybal worked for the Lab first as a construction worker building the barracks for Project Y. Later he became a bus driver, bringing in janitors and cooks from throughout the surrounding valleys up to the hill to work every day. My maternal great-grandmother María Aurelia Luján was a maid cleaning houses for the scientist's wives. Before this, my great-grandparents lived off the land. Sustenance agriculture.

They said the mountains burned purple.

Stories. Stories of vecinos being transported up the hill on flatbed trucks with wooden benches installed in the back. My great-grandfather at the wheel. Stories of the same vecinos who were evicted from the Pajarito Plateau crying as the truck made its way up the hill, forced to provide menial labor in their former home.

My maternal grandmother María Graciola Roybal and her sisters, my great aunts, were primed in high school to be assistants and secretaries at the Lab with classes in typing and shorthand. One of my great-aunts worked there for 17 years. My grandmother retired from the Lab, working there all her life. Her starting wage was one dollar and sixty-three cents an hour.

Plutonium. Uranium. Bon Ami.

Geiger counters. Asbestos protection suits. Radiation.

My dad worked at the Lab for a few years in the late 1970s. Thirty five years later, my dad, like so many others,was diagnosed with cancer. He got sick from toxic chemicals and radioactive nuclear materials that he was exposed to during his time working at the Lab.

They said the mountains burned purple. And the people are sick.

When my dad got sick, he qualified for the Energy Employees Occupational Illness Compensation Program Act.

The government provided "free lifetime health benefits" to a terminally ill cancer patient, wage loss, and a compensation of between $100,000 and $250,000 dollars under the EEOICPA.

> *What did he die of?*
> *What are the last four digits of his social security number?*

But what about the spouses of workers who were contaminated? Who are contaminated? Will my mom get sick? Stories of government workers pushing barrels of toxic nuclear waste off of cliffs to the valleys below. Burying nuclear waste nearby. When my family went fishing in Cochiti lake when I was a child, we didn't know the high levels of contamination. The land is sick. The water is sick. Will I get sick?

A copy of his death certificate.

There were forest fires in the area a few years back and the locals say the mountains burned purple.

A copy of your birth certificate.

I know there is a cancer cluster that no one is talking about. Four of my great-aunts and great- uncles died from cancer and my grandfather has cancer too.

Lung cancer. Stomach cancer. Pancreatic cancer. Colon cancer. The lab is built on a super volcano.

Employment Information from the Department of Social Security showing his time at the Lab.

When I tell my family's story of Los Alamos, people want me to tell my story in relation to the famous scientists, Oppenhiemer, Groves, Dudley, Teller, Fermi. How did my ancestors know them? Did they work for them? Which scientists' houses did they clean? But I am not interested in the scientists or the menial labor my Granmita provided for some scientist's wife. I am interested in the untold stories, my family's stories, and their experiences of the Lab.

> *From U.S. Department of Labor:*
>
> *Dear Mr. Montoya,*
>
> *We have received your claim under the Energy Employees Occupational Illness Compensation Program Act. Your claim has been assigned to a Claims Examiner for review.*

My dad is considered a Cold War Patriot. What about my great aunts María Adelia and María Evelina who grew up eating beans and squash grown in the valley beneath the creation of the Atomic bomb? Where were their payouts when they died of stomach cancer?

And why is this story always told by people from NYC? People who never touched the earth that is now sick for generations to come. The earth that burns purple. The land, water, and people, _my_ people, _my_ family are scarred and sick from Project Y, the Manhattan Project, the Atomic Bomb.

> *On May 22, 2013 the Final Adjudication Branch issued a Final Decision accepting Johnny S. Montoya's claim for colorectal adenocarcinoma metastatic to the liver under Part B and Part E. On October 15, 2013, we issued a letter accepting his claim for metastatic cancer to the lungs.*

They said the mountains burned purple. The people are sick, the land and water are sick.

In 2004, after a handful of lawsuits and sixty years later, Congress authorized a $10 million Pajarito Plateau Homesteaders Compensation Fund to pay the descendants of the homesteaders evicted from the Pajarito Plateau. The government under paid Nuevomexicanos for the land in the 1940s- Nuevomexicanos, including my great-grandparents received $7-15/acre which was much less than the $225/acre paid to the White owned Los Alamos Ranch School.

As a direct descendent of Sofía Vigil and Norberto Roybal, my maternal grandfather received an undisclosed pay out.

Before my Dad died, he was compensated by the U.S. Government under the Energy Employees Occupational Illness Compensation Program Act or the EEOICPA. The government also paid for his terminal cancer treatment.

They said the mountains burned purple. The people are sick, the land and water are sick.

In case you are curious, I did not get a cent from any of these government pay offs.

In all honesty, I'd rather have my dad back.

---

* The italics in Pajarito reflect direct quotes from various government documents and direct correspondence with the Montoya family.

Resource

Gómez, Myrriah. "Nuclear Nuevo México: Colonialism and the Effects of the Nuclear Industrial Complex on Nuevomexicanos." The University of Arizona Press, 2022.

UNSPOKEN

Silent stories. Unspoken stories. Stories whose time has not yet come.

Sometimes it isn't the right time to share a story. Perhaps time needs to pass, the seasons need to change, or the story needs time to simmer, marinate. Some stories are too precious and fragile to share.

Fragile stories are like hummingbird eggs or delicate glass that might break with a breath. Some stories held close to the heart are only shared between one or two people. Other stories are too painful to share. Silence is the dam that holds in the flood of emotional wounds and pain that either cannot or does not want to be released.

Silent stories. Unspoken stories. Stories whose time has not yet come.

I left home at eighteen years old with stars in my eyes. Eager to get away from Albuquerque's cold winds that blow for too many months out of the year. I traversed down the Jornada del Muerto towards the Sonoran desert eager to escape my silent and unspoken stories.

CÓMO ERES

A Sonoran borderlands love story

When I arrived in Tucson at the age of eighteen, my plan was to attend the university, dance as much as I possibly could and then journey off to live in a place with water. As a child of the desert, I thought it would be great to live near an ocean. California. Or possibly Hawai'i. But destiny had other plans. After undergrad came graduate school and then an offer to teach as an adjunct professor at the University of Arizona in the Mexican American Studies Department, an offer that my twentyfive-year-old self could not deny.

About a month before I was to begin that new job, I attended a birthday party that changed my life. At the old Z's pizza in Tucson, Arizona, I sat next to the nephew of my dear friend Ximena. After I sat down, I soon began chatting with her nephew Salvador, who, like other Mexican Salvador's has the nickname Chava (and yes, it also means girl, I digress). I soon discovered Chava and I shared the same love of dance. We began to go out dancing together at least once, sometimes twice, a week and we would also invite each other to attend local dance classes together. Don't worry, my friend and her nephews are the same age, you know, large Catholic families. This went on for a couple years, I would teach during the week and go out dancing with Chava every Saturday night .

Time passed and Chava moved away. Chava was an undocumented immigrant. Although his grandfather, Salvador Mújica-Cortez, was born in Morenci, Arizona, Chava and his father, whose last name was since changed to Martínez, but that is another story for another time... they were born in Cananea, México. You see, three generations ago, the southern border was much more fluid than it is now, and people and families moved more freely, including copper miners. Chava's grandfathers and great-grandfathers were copper miners. In the early 1990s, Chava came with his family to Tucson. He was eleven years old. Then, Chava's grandfather, the U.S.-born citizen who was in the process of sponsoring the family's immigration, unexpectedly passed away. The process stopped. Because of immigration laws at that time, the family was left with no option to immigrate. Undocumented.

After working construction for a few years post-college, Chava left Tucson in search of a different type of work, which he found with a Chinese company in California who employed undocumented laborers in IT positions. We remained friends, texting and chatting on the phone, and we would go out dancing whenever he would come to town, which was not often.

In 2007, my cousin got married in San Diego. I

headed to California a few days early to visit my friend Chava in L.A., and something clicked. We became more than friends. A whirlwind romance and a shotgun wedding in Vegas shortly followed. My dear friend Ximena became my Tía Ximena and I haven't left the desert for the ocean. At least not yet.

QUERENCIA

And now for the stories that are still being written. The stories that are unfolding right at this very moment. The stories that are happening right now, today.

For me, this is the story of my small family. The story of me, Chava and our son, who we lovingly call Buddy. He really dislikes that name now that he is a teen.

Buddy is an only child who bears the names of his

grandfathers. Long names with lots of syllables that he is finally beginning to grow into.

Buddy is very fortunate. When he was born, he met one of his great-great-grandmothers, three of his great-grandmothers, and one of his great-grandfathers.

Although Buddy lives in the borderlands of Tucson in the space between his mother's homelands of New Mexico and his father's hometown of Cananea, Sonora, he visits his New Mexican family for a week every summer and spends many weekends with his Mexican grandparents who live in Tucson. Buddy knows all about his deep, deep Nuevomexicano roots and his many Nuevomexicano ancestors. Sometimes he asks me questions about his Mexican roots and ancestors, questions that I cannot answer.

In the borderlands in Tucson, Buddy is sometimes unfairly asked to take sides in the tortilla, posole, and tamale wars that happen in our home. But we all agree that New Mexico's chile is the best!

Every December, Buddy and I make farolitos (or

luminarias for the *Burqueños*), natillas, and New Mexico style tortillas and posole. But our most favorite thing to make is biscochitos using his great-great-grandmother's recipe. Biscochitos was one of the things my granmita taught me to make after I learned Spanish. She had no recipe for the cookies, she would eyeball the ingredients, which made it really challenging for me to write down her technique and turn it into a recipe! One year, Buddy's grandmother and great-grandmother came to visit around the holidays and four generations of Nuevomexicanos gathered in my kitchen, kneaded masa, and made our granmita's biscochitos.

Buddy. *'Jito. Hijo de mi alma.* My child of the deserts. My monsoon baby. Time is sacred and I am so blessed to share it with you. Remember the stories. Remember your roots. Remember who you are. And when I am gone, I hope you remember and share some of our stories with your children and grandchildren.

I am Yvonne Montoya. I am the mother of Salvador Martínez-Montoya. And this is my story.

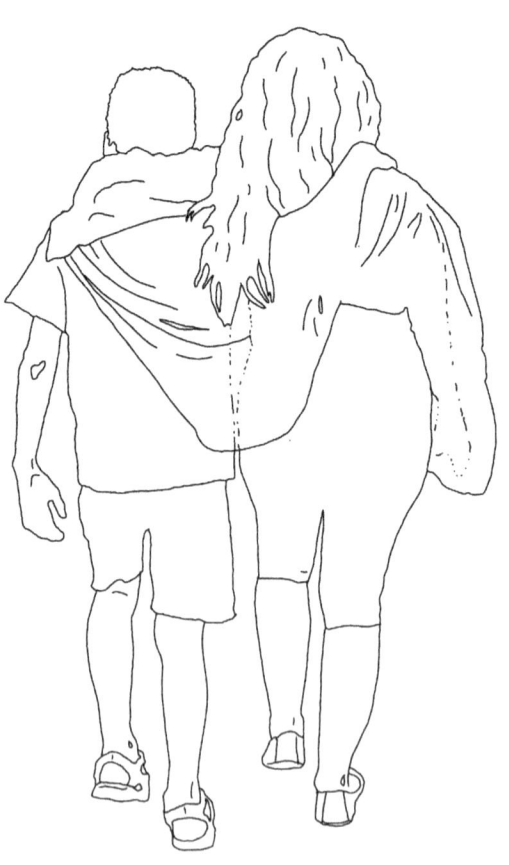

ACKNOWLEDGEMENT

Thank you to Michele Orduña for the lunches where I brainstormed and thought through these writings in conversation with you. And for reading a version of the drafts.

Thank you to Michelle Marji for editing the stories, monologues.

Thank you to theater directors Mary Ann Gale and Dr. Erica Acevedo-Ontiveros, and acting coach Dr. Ana Cornide who helped me (an untrained actor) get these monologues performance ready.

Thank you to Wesley Fawcett Creigh, digital animator who adapted video stills for the illustrations in this book. Thank you Wesley for designing the cover of this book and helping me with typesetting.

Thank you to Baylie MacRae because I could not do any of this without you. Baylie MacRae is also the photographer who took the head shot on the cover of the book. The headshot appears courtesy of *Safos* Dance Theatre.

Thank you to Dr. Myrriah Gómez for being the unofficial dramaturg for *Pajarito* and showing so much support for this work.

Thank you to Ruby Morales for using my words in draft form as inspiration for your choreography. Thank you Ruby for beautifully bringing the stories of my ancestors and great-great-grandmothers to life.

Thank you to Liz Lerman for encouraging me to perform the *Pajarito* and *Deslenguadas* monologues on stage.

Thank you to Buddy for letting me share our story.

Thank you to my husband Salvador "Chava" Martínez-Baldenegro. Without your support, there would be no *Stories from Home* or *Safos* Dance

Theatre.

And thank you to *Safos* Dance Theatre for supporting my goal to publish these writings.

❆ ❆ ❆

Program Notes for *Stories from Home*

From the Director

Stories from Home is the physical embodiment of the oral traditions of Northern New Mexico. This collection of dances embodies stories inspired by my father and were created for my son in honor of our ancestors, our querenica, and our deep deep Nuevomexicano roots. This is an artistic interpretation of my family's histories and stories inspired by and based on, but not beholden to, historical accuracies as time is not linear in this storytelling experience. I am delighted to share my family's stories and cultural traditions with you.

Stories From Home Design Team

Artistic Director: Yvonne Montoya
Choreography: Yvonne Montoya et al
Lighting Designer : Clint Bryson
Digital Animator : Wesley Fawcett Creigh
Costume Designers: Kelsey Vidic, Mary Leopo
Stage Manager: Dr. Erica Acevedo Ontiveros
Music: Samuel Peña et al

Original Cast

Dancers: Ruby Morales, Esteban Rosales, Lauren Jimenez, Zarina Mendoza Orduño, David Bernal-Fuentes
Swing Cast: Delia Ibañez
Rehearsal Assistants: Delia Ibañez, Baylie MacRae
Additional Performers: Yvonne Montoya, Salvador "Buddy" Martínez-Montoya

2025-2026 Cast

Dancers: Ruby Morales, José José Arrieta Cuesta, Angela Bass, Vincent Chávez, Madeline McDonald
Swing Cast: Esteban Rosales, Zarina Mendoza Orduño
Apprentices: Martín Quintana, Isis América Tovar Laborín
Additional Performers: Yvonne Montoya, Salvador "Buddy" Martínez-Montoya
Costume Technican: Alisha Patel

The Dances

Preshow Music: Lone Piñon

ACT ONE

Tecolote
Choreographer & Text: Yvonne Montoya
Costume: Kelsey Vidic
Music: " El Tecolotito" by Lone Piñon

Lone Piñon's 2017 arrangement of a traditional song as sung by Ricardo Archuleta of Antonito, CO on August 4, 1940 for Juan Rael, whose recordings are available online through the Library of Congress. Vocals: Jordan Wax, Lia Martinez, Shae Fiol

Tecolote Redux*
Choreography: Yvonne Montoya
Music: Samuel Peña
Costume: Kelsey Vidic

Mestiza Mulata de Analco
Artistic Director, Text & Performer: Yvonne Montoya
Choreographer: Ruby Morales
Costume: Kelsey Vidic

Siglos. Sueños. Sefarad.
Choreographer: Yvonne Montoya
Music: "Morena Me Yaman" by Edith Saint-Mard/ Michael Grebil/Bernard Mouton/Thomas Baete, Vincent Libert
Costume: Kelsey Vidic

Deslenguadas
Choreographer: Yvonne Montoya
Music: "Deslenguadas" by Samuel Peña Voice with recordings of María Graciola Roybal, María Adelia Roybal Baldock, María Aurelia Luján, and a recreation of María Diolanda García's oral history by Yvonne Montoya
Costumes: Mary Leopo, Kelsey Vidic
Text: Yvonne Montoya with excerpts of Gloria Anzaldúa's *La Nueva Mestiza's* "How to Tame a Wild Tongue"

Braceros
Choreography: Yvonne Montoya
Music: "Braceros" by Samuel Peña
Voice recording of Juan "Johnny" Montoya by Yvonne Montoya
Costume: Mary Leopo

ACT TWO

Pajarito
Choreography, Text & Performance: Yvonne Montoya
Music: "Pajarito" by Samuel Peña
Costume: Mary Leopo

Unspoken
Choreography: Yvonne Montoya
Music: "De Casa" by Samuel Peña
Costume: Mary Leopo

Cómo eres
Choreography: Yvonne Montoya
Sonora Bronco Choreography: Isis América Tovar Laborín
Music: "Sobre mis pies" written by Isidro Chavez Espinoza used by permission of Peermusic III, Ltd. All rights reserved.
Costume: Kelsey Vidic

Querencia
Choreography, Text & Performance: Yvonne Montoya
Music & Performance: Salvador Martínez-Montoya
Dance films: Dominic AZ Bonuccelli
Dance film music: Excerpts of "Monólogo para Cello" by Maria Granillo performed by Edgardo Espinosa, Musette in D Major, BWV Anh. 126 from Anna Magdalena Bach Klavierbüchlein, 1725 performed by Salvador Martínez-Montoya, and "Walking: A Soundscape" by Yvonne Montoya with Salvador Martínez-Montoya
Costumes: Mary Leopo

Music and movement inspired by the traditional Nuevomexicano Bailes de Salón and the traditional Spanish language music of Northern New Mexico including **la Varceliana, la Camila, la Cuna**, and the **Matachines**. Special thank you to **Salvador Martínez-Baldenegro** and **Lucy Salazar**.

Tecolote Redux is performed four times throughout the show. Each solo dance is different. Because the choreographer, composer, and costume design is the same for all for dances, the credits are only included once in this program. The *Tecolote Redux a*re the dances with no written narrative that accompany them. These four short solos are performed inbetween every two dances with narratives.

❈ ❈ ❈

Support From Funders

Stories from Home has been in development for many years. The following funders, organizations, people, and artist residencies supported the creation of this work over the years.

National Association of Latino Arts and Cultures

Stories from Home is supported in part by the National Association of Latino Arts and Cultures through a grant from the NALAC Fund for the Arts.

Arizona Community Foundation Community Support Grant

This project was supported by a grant from the Arizona Community Foundation. Established in 1978, the Arizona Community Foundation is a statewide family of charitable funds supported by thousands of Arizonans. Since inception, ACF has awarded over $1 billion in grants, scholarships, and loans to nonprofit organizations, schools, and government agencies. More information is available at azfoundation.org.

National Performance Network Creation Fund Grant

Safos Dance Theatre was awarded the 2022 National Performance Network Creation Fund for Yvonne Montoya's Stories from Home. This grant was awarded in collaboration with two co-commissioners, GALA Hispanic Theatre (Washington, DC) and Su Teatro (Denver, CO). Thank you NPN, Su Teatro, and GALA Hispanic Theatre for your support! Creation and Development Fund is made possible with support from the Doris Duke Charitable Foundation, the Mellon Foundation, the National Endowment for the Arts (a federal agency), and co-commissioners.

This project is supported by the National Performance Network (NPN) Documentation & Storytelling Initiative with funding from the Doris Duke Foundation and the National Endowment for the Arts (a federal agency). For more information, visit www.npnweb.org.

National Endowment for the Arts Grants for Arts Projects

Safos Dance Theatre was awarded the 2022 Grant for Arts Projects for Yvonne Montoya's *Stories from Home*. This project is one of 14 projects awarded funding in Arizona in 2022. Thank you NEA for your support!

The MAP Fund

Yvonne Montoya is a 2020 MAP Fund Grantee for *Stories from Home*. She is among 171 performing artists and arts organizations grantees who received funding from all over the country in 2020. The MAP Fund is supported by the Doris Duke Charitable Foundation and the Andrew W. Mellon Foundation. Thank you MAP for your support.

New England Foundation for the Arts National Dance Project

Yvonne Montoya is a 2020 NEFA National Dance Project Production Grant recipient for the creation and production of *Stories from Home*. She is honored to be the first Arizona-based artist to receive this award. Montoya and the Stories from Home team is very excited about what this means for Arizona-based dance artists, and Nuevomexicna and Xicana stories from the Southwest being shared nationally. Congratulations to all of the grant recipients and finalists! This grant is made possible by the New

England Foundation for the Arts' National Dance Project, with lead funding from the Doris Duke Charitable Foundation and The Andrew W. Mellon Foundation. Thank you NEFA!

Arizona Commission on the Arts

Stories from Home is supported in part by the Arizona Commission on the Arts which receives support from the State of Arizona and the National Endowment for the Arts.

Arts Foundation for Tucson and Southern Arizona

Stories from Home is supported by the Arts Foundation for Tucson and Southern Arizona. Funded in part by The National Endowment for the Arts, City of Tucson, and Pima County

Arizona State University

Stories from Home is supported by Projecting All Voices, a program of Arizona State University Herberger Institute for Design and the Arts, and Arizona State University Gammage. The Projecting All Voices Fellowship, a program of the Studio for Creativity, Place and Equitable Communities at Arizona State University Herberger Institute for Design and the Arts.

The Kennedy Center

Parts of *Stories from Home* was developed as a part

of the Kennedy Center Office Hours Page to Stage Residency program at the REACH.

ABOUT THE AUTHOR

Yvonne Marie Montoya

Yvonne Montoya is a mother, choreographer, writer, and the founding director of Safos Dance Theatre. Based in Tucson, AZ and originally from Albuquerque, NM, her work is grounded in and inspired by the landscapes, languages, cultures, and aesthetics of the U.S. Southwest.

Though most well-known in the U.S. Southwest, her choreography has been staged across the United States and in Guatemala, and her dance films screened, at Queens University of Charlotte, N.C., and the University of Exeter (U.K.) Under her direction, Safos Dance Theatre won the Tucson Pima Arts Council's Lumie Award for Emerging Organization in 2015.

From 2017-2018 Montoya was a Post-Graduate Fellow in Dance at Arizona State University, where she founded and organized the inaugural Dance in the Desert. From 2019-2020, Montoya was a

Kennedy Center Citizen Artist Fellow, a member of the 2019-2020 Dance/USA Fellowships to Artists pilot program, and a 2021-2022 Southwest Folk Alliance Plain View Fellow. Montoya was a recipient of the 2019 National Association of Latino Arts and Cultures (NALAC) POD grant, the 2020 MAP Fund Award, and the first Arizona-based artist to receive the 2020 New England Foundation for the Arts (NEFA) National Dance Project Production Grant. Montoya won the Arizona Creative Excellence Award at the 2021 Arizona Drive-In Dance Film Festival. In 2022, her company Safos Dance Theatre received the National Performance Network Creation Fund Grant and the National Endowment for the Arts Grants for Arts Project Grant for her piece Stories from Home. Stories from Home premiered at GALA Hispanic Theatre in Washington, D.C. in October 2023 and is currently touring the Southwest. Montoya was also featured in KQED's If Cities Could Dance and KNME's ¡COLORES!.

Montoya is also a writer and has been published by University of Arizona Press, Border Lore, Revista Música del Sur, Chicana Motherwork, El Mundo Zurdo, and Chamisa: A Journal of Literary, Performance, and Visual Arts of the Greater Southwest. She is the founder of Montoya Publishing and the lead writer for MPA Project Travels. For more information, visit www.yvonnemontoya.co

BOOKS BY THIS AUTHOR

Reflections: Writings From The Motherhood And Performing Arts Project

Reflections is the collection of the original blog posts and writings from the Motherhood and Performing Arts (MPA) Project. Motherhood and the Performing Arts (MPA) Project was a multidisciplinary mother and son art project that took place in Tucson, Arizona between July 2015 - December 2016. The book reflects on the challenges one mother faced as she worked as a dancer, choreographer, and director at a small contemporary dance company in Tucson, AZ. This journey is an honest, and sometimes painful, look at the past into the joys and challenges of balancing motherhood with a career in dance.

Publication of Reflections: Writings from the Motherhood and Performing Arts Project marks the 10th anniversary of the MPA Project. The book documents and shares the blog posts that are no longer available online.

My Stories From Home: A Family Memory Book

Do you ever find yourself longing to preserve your family stories? To document the memories, voices, and histories that connect one generation to the next? Inspired by Yvonne Montoya's Stories from Home, this personal journal is your gateway to uncovering your roots and celebrating your family's unique narrative.

Packed with thoughtful prompts, this journal guides you through documenting your stories. Each page invites you to reflect, record, and write your story of home.

Whether you're nurturing a family tradition, cultivating your querencia, or simply looking for a way to capture and celebrate your roots, this journal will be one you and yours keep coming back to for years to come.

STORIES FROM HOME

www.ingramcontent.com/pod-product-compliance
Lightning Source LLC
Chambersburg PA
CBHW071121160426
43196CB00013B/2663